How to Understand Men
Through Their Dogs

How to Understand Men Through Their Dogs

Wendy Diamond

Sterling Publishing Co., Inc.
NEW YORK

DEDICATION

To all those lucky people who find love
through man's best friend.

Library of Congress Cataloging-in-Publication Data Available

2 4 6 8 10 9 7 5 3 1

Published by Sterling Publishing Co., Inc.
387 Park Avenue South, New York, NY 10016
© 2006 by Wendy Diamond
Distributed in Canada by Sterling Publishing
c/o Canadian Manda Group, 165 Dufferin Street
Toronto, Ontario, Canada M6K 3H6
Distributed in the United Kingdom by GMC Distribution Services
Castle Place, 166 High Street, Lewes, East Sussex, England BN7 1XU
Distributed in Australia by Capricorn Link (Australia) Pty. Ltd.
P.O. Box 704, Windsor, NSW 2756, Australia

Printed in China

Sterling ISBN-13: 978-1-4027-3096-2
ISBN-10: 1-4027-3096-9

For information about custom editions, special sales, premium and
corporate purchases, please contact Sterling Special Sales
Department at 800-805-5489 or specialsales@sterlingpub.com.

CONTENTS

INTRODUCTION

W E ALL HAVE THE PASSIONATE desire to meet the ideal mate. In the United States alone there are eighty-five million singles looking for the right partner. My own quest for finding the perfect man led me to discover the similarities between men and their dogs. My beautiful white Maltese, Lucky, is a dog magnet! I've met many interesting men and their different breeds of canines thanks to Lucky. As founder and editorial director of *Animal Fair*, a lifestyle magazine for animal lovers, my possibilities for meeting and dating men with different breeds of dogs through my work, travel, and adventures with my own dog have been unending. I wanted to share my insights with curious and optimistic women around the world.

How to Understand Men Through Their Dogs is the ultimate dating guidebook for singles of all persuasions, those living with or married to men with dogs, those who have a friend with a dog, or anyone searching for Mr. Right! In Chapter One I provide readers with a brief history of canines, past, present, and future. There are more than sixty-eight million dogs in the United States, and at the end of half of those leashes are men. Dog is man's loyal best friend! Since men naturally identify with dogs, in Chapter Two I have humorously explored finding the common links and shared personality traits between men and their dogs. Through my own amusing experiences and extensive research, I composed a compilation of what women can expect from thirty-two different types of men who own certain breeds. Is Irish Setter Man always going to be at the pub? Will you be able to stay in the race with Mr. Greyhound? Are Rottweilers really dangerous? So many questions, so few answers . . . until now. It's common knowledge that both men and dogs have the tendency to stray. Once you find the perfect breed of man for you, how do you keep him from scratching at the front door to get out? Chapter Three includes comical, instructive training tips. Through these training methods, you'll become the master of your relationship. Although I find that every breed is different, the training tips do work, and I personally suggest that you try them right from the start of your romance to promote longevity and happiness. Does your Golden Retriever Man jump all over you in public? Are you tired of cleaning up Mr. Cocker Spaniel's clothes from the floor, back of the chair, or end of the bed? Is the Dober-Man's overprotective barking in public getting out of control? My specific tried-and-true training tips will give you the skills you need to curb your man while still having great fun!

I thought, What's a book about dating without success stories? In Chapter Four I've included true circumstances in which dogs have played an integral part in bringing couples together with positive results and in which dogs have altered the fates of different people and situations, probably unintentionally but still constructively. The dogs in these success stories act as innocent muses, using leashes as conduits to create divine intervention and happy endings. These stories are doggone comical—and real. I'm so positive that you'll be inspired by the stories that in Chapter Five I've provided a list of places where you can purchase different breeds or adopt mutts and strays.

I'm still single, dating, and looking to find the ideal man—and true love. I'm only halfway through dating the breeds of men listed in my book! My dog, Lucky, has put the bark out for me among her canine crowd at the dog run, so I'm sure it won't be long until I find Mr. Right. Let this entertaining guidebook help you figure out more about the men in your life through the dog(s) they own. I'm confident that you'll get as much enjoyment dating the different breeds, using the training tips, and reading the success stories as I did writing this book. And when you do meet the perfect man, what a lucky dog!

CHAPTER ONE

History of Dogs

*"The greater love is a mother's; then comes a dog's;
then a sweetheart's."*

Polish proverb

ave you ever wondered where the word *dog* originates? It's a shortened version of the Latin term *Canis* (dog) *familiaris* (domestic). Scientists discovered in 1997 through new molecular genetic techniques that man's best friend is actually much older than first thought. Men are like dogs, identify with dogs, and share a long history with dogs. Dogs can be genetically traced possibly as far back as one hundred thousand years or more. Originally it was believed that dogs were only twenty thousand years old. The new scientific discovery confirms that dogs evolved from wolves. The Latin term *Canis familiaris* was changed in the 1990s to *Canis lupus* (wolf) *familiaris*. Maybe this latest scientific information explains your dog's—and your man's—wild behavior and howling at the full moon!

The first recorded history of humankind's relationships with dogs began twenty thousand years ago. Prehistoric men first began to use dogs for hunting, so women really can't blame today's men for their instinct to flirt—they've got thousands of years of the game and chase behind them! It wasn't until five thousand to seven thousand years ago that dogs were domesticated as important protectors and guards, and worked alongside humans. Various Roman and Asiatic dog bloodlines were spread among local dogs throughout Europe during different invasions and wars. Breeding and training became important for improved hunting, herding, and guarding skills.

Throughout history, man's closest companion, his dog, traveled everywhere with him, leading to the expansion of many breeds from Europe to the Middle East to the United States. And you think your man gets around! Some breeds gained and lost popularity at critical times throughout civilization because of royal favoritism, the Crusades and Inquisition, war, famine, plagues, and usefulness.

Luckily, during the 1900s various organizations were created to prevent breeds from going extinct, and many shelters were established to promote finding homeless and stray dogs permanent homes (see Chapter Five for a list of organizations).

We don't want to lose any of the darling breeds and mutts that have become such a cherished part of our daily lives!

Dogs have served many purposes throughout time. They were used for hunting, protecting, and herding, and as quiet confidants. Many presidents, celebrities, and successful businesspeople find solace in the unconditional love dogs provide. In the earlier twentieth century, when a man was called a "dog," it meant that he was a scoundrel or cad. In modern pop culture the term "dog," or "dawg," denotes positive social identification for a man from his inner circle.

How to Understand Men Through Their Dogs takes this one step further by providing a dating guidebook for women, defining the men in their lives through the dogs they own. I foresee a new wave in pop culture emerging: A man won't be vaguely called a "dog" anymore—he'll be humorously defined and nicknamed by the breed or mutt he owns! He'll now be a "Dober-Man," a "Lab Man," "Mr. Beagle," "Mutt Man," and so on.

Here are some fun historic facts about dogs: The world's largest, heaviest, and longest dog was recorded in 1989. An Old English Mastiff named Zorba weighed 343 pounds and was 8 feet 3 inches long from nose to tail! Can you imagine feeding this dog every day? The world's smallest dog was a tiny Yorkie from Blackburn, England. Fully grown, it was only 2.5 inches tall and 3.75 inches long and weighed only 4 ounces. Watch where you step! The oldest recorded reliable age for a blessed dog is twenty-nine years, five months for a Queensland "heeler" (Australian cattle dog) named Bluey in Victoria, Australia. That's more than 206 years old in human years!

Ladies, we should celebrate the scientists who proved that all the different breeds of dogs are direct descendants of the wolf. Wolves are monogamous and mate with one partner for life. The historical facts favor women who desire a blissful lifetime commitment with just one man!

CHAPTER TWO

Dog Breeds and Men

*"I wonder if other dogs think poodles
are members of a weird religious cult."*

RITA RUDNER

Is it by chance that a man chooses a Great Dane or poodle as his constant companion and best friend? Or is it because they share similar personality traits and he can specifically identify with a certain breed? We'll look at the most popular breeds to gain insight into their male human companions. Of course, like many people, not all dogs and men are purely one breed or another, so I've included a mutt description. If you know that your man's mutt is half German shepherd and half collie, read both of these descriptions to get a better understanding of his more complex personality. And have fun using this chapter to try to figure out exactly what type of mutt your man is!

This guide is for all of you who are single, dating, committed, or merely curious to figure out whether your male companion is sincerely loyal and true blue, marriage material, a pack hound, or a hopeless roamer too distracted to commit. You'll gain insight as to what you can expect from a date with a certain breed, the profession he might choose, whether children are in his future, and celebrity examples to identify with.

Next, I take you one step further and let you know what you can expect from a certain breed when he's feeling a bit naughty and mischievous. Does an Irish Setter honestly stay out all night at the pub? Is a Rottweiler's bark really worse than his bite? Can a Greyhound slow down enough to commit? Inside, you'll find essential answers and much more to help you decide whether you can handle a certain breed's wilder side.

We've all heard the saying "You can't teach an old dog new tricks." I give you constructive hints on how to help each different breed work on certain personality weaknesses! Since certain breeds resist constructive criticism and learning new ways of behaving, this chapter gives you the necessary inside information you need to curb your man! Have fun discussing each breed with girlfriends over Sunday brunch, with coworkers during lunch, with your mother or sisters over dinner, or even with your special man while walking his dog to the local dog run! Here we go!

Akita

Personality

Sushi, anyone? Mr. Akita's heritage stems from the exotic land of Japan. His ancestors didn't set foot (or should I say paw?) in America until 1937. This samurai man is quiet, strong, independent, and stubborn. He's not above getting into a verbal or physical wrestling match if he thinks those he loves are in danger. He can overreact and be overprotective. Therefore, if you're a social animal, this isn't the breed for you. If you enjoy being a geisha girl in search of a devoted homebody and protective family man, look no farther. The Akita Man is loyal beyond belief.

The ideal first date would be a quiet dinner for two at home with a table set with origami, tempura, a little sake to relax him, and a large bowl of good conversation. Besides being physically powerful, he's also intelligent and well-mannered. Mr. Akita needs a large dose of daily physical exercise, so take off that kimono already, put on your jogging shoes, and encourage him to take a run through the park with you. The perfect profession for this man is banker, international business executive, recording studio owner, restaurant owner, or jazz musician. For example, *Saturday Night Live* legend and Blues

Brother Dan Aykroyd is an Akita Man who loves to howl the blues and jazz. Evander Holyfield channeled his Akita samurai fighting energy into boxing. Elvis Stojko is an ice-skating Akita Olympian. Akita Men feel especially feisty in cooler temperatures. Your winter months will be active, warm, and stimulating. This man will make you feel loved no matter what season it is!

Naughty Dog

The Akita Man can be very domineering. His constant need to guard and protect can make him think his way is the only way, for the good of all. He's leery of new people, which can make it difficult for a newcomer to enter the clan.

New Trick

Tell Mr. Akita to *lighten up*! He can be very standoffish when meeting people or in social situations. He doesn't trust anyone outside of his inner circle. Slowly get him used to the idea that everyone isn't his enemy. By example, you can show him that it's safe to let his guard down every now and then!

Basset Hound

Personality

Do you remember the affectionate cartoon character Pepé Le Pew? He was the lovable French skunk who, once he caught the scent of a woman, pursued her to the ends of the earth proclaiming his undying love. Mr. Basset Hound's personality is very similar! He'll sniff you out with a deliberate and focused pursuit. In other words—he'll be hot on your trail! After Mr. Basset Hound has tracked you down, you'll find he's a well-mannered, soulful, and sensitive man with a playful nature. His quirky and goofy mannerisms can keep you chuckling to yourself all day long.

One of his favorite activities is trail hiking. The Basset Hound Man takes pride in his reputation for being a talented hiker. Here's the catch: He becomes so involved in following one trail to its end, without looking at other possible trails, that he gets easily lost. Head for the hills with him but study the trail map before leaving. Give him subtle directions and options without being obvious about it. This approach also applies to any road trips you decide to take with Mr. Basset Hound. Your target destination might be Boston, but pack your swimsuit because you might end up in Miami!

The Basset Hound Man's desired occupation might be travel agent, rock climber, architect, highway designer, engineer, door-to-door salesman, or postman. *Dirty Harry* Basset Hound Clint Eastwood hikes the trails of Carmel. Don't get discouraged if navigating your highway to love with the Basset Hound Man becomes a maze of winding twists, turns, detours, and roadblocks. Take heart! He's well worth the hassle. Keep your eye on the ultimate destination point—the altar!

Naughty Dog

The Basset Hound Man will treat your possessions as if they belong to him. Unintentionally, he can be destructive with others' belongings. He'll break your favorite toys without meaning to. And when you try to discuss the situation, he'll get defensive and stubborn, making it even more difficult for you to reclaim your territory!

New Trick

The Basset Hound Man needs regular daily exercise. He tends to move slowly, and he has a weak back that requires strengthening. Explain to him that preventative medicine is the best policy and will thwart worse back problems when he's an older hound.

Beagle

Personality

Watch out—he's a heartbreaker, ladies! The Beagle Man possesses the lethal combination of being both handsome and sensitive. He's a fox-hound! You'll be mesmerized by him at the first hello. Don't be fooled by his sweet, shy nature, because he's quite courageous, he has the stamina of ten huskies, and he knows who's boss—at least he thinks so (wink-wink).

Mr. Beagle is a social creature and loves being one of the guys. If he wants to hang out with his buddies on the weekends, don't feel left out or neglected. Instead, suggest that you and your girlfriends meet up with him and his posse at a happening nightclub or your local park for a Sunday afternoon game of touch football or baseball. He's very high strung, so any physical activity the two of you can do together in and out of the bedroom—all the better for your relationship. Mr. Beagle will have a career as an ambulance driver, chef, train conductor, firefighter, or professor. Howling Beagle Man Barry Manilow croons about finding romance at the Copacabana and sings endless love songs. The Beagle Man has the inherent potential to be perfect marriage material. He wants children and thrives in a steady home life.

Breakfast, lunch, and dinner are sacred times of day for the Beagle Man. Get your culinary skills in tip-top shape, because this man can eat, and eat, and eat!

Naughty Dog

Mr. Beagle loves to yap, bark, and vocalize. If you go to powder your nose at dinner, when you return to your seat, don't be surprised to find Mr. Beagle engaged in an endless conversation with the stranger sitting at the next table. It's wonderful that he's so outgoing, but his constant chattering might get exhausting. Once you regain his full attention, he'll charm his way right over to your plate and take a big bite of whatever he desires.

New Trick

You're going to have to be tolerant when housebreaking this man! Mr. Beagle is stubborn and slow to change. If you charm him with fun and laughter, before you know it you'll have him eating out of the palm of your hand, not off your plate.

Bernese Mountain Dog

Personality

If country living is the life for you, then so is the Bernese Mountain Man! He's a calm, loyal, and sensitive man who loves the great outdoors. Mr. Bernese Mountain Man is very muscular and strong and likes daily exercise and manual labor. He doesn't survive very well in urban and city apartment dwellings—too many people make him nervous. So does hot weather; he excels in cooler climates. He'll perpetually choose open pastures over crowded restaurants and cafés. His ancestors lived in the Swiss Alps, and the open air gets his juices flowing.

This man has a built-in people phobia and will spend all of his time exclusively with his girlfriend, wife, or family. Strangers are personae non gratae as far as he's concerned! He's wonderful father material and a protective provider. If you're a high-powered career woman with a healthy income and a desire to have children without quitting your job, Mr. Bernese Mountain Man is the perfect stay-at-home dad! No stuffy offices or boardrooms for this man! Instead the Bernese Mountain Man prefers a profession as a farmer, agriculturist, landscaper, consultant with a home office, writer, producer, horticulturist, or soccer coach. Passionate Bernese Mountain

Man Robert De Niro has starred in the movies *Wag the Dog*, *Mad Dog and Glory*, and *Deer Hunter*. He frequently escapes the city for his widespread mountain ranch. If you desire birds chirping in the morning instead of horns honking, and fresh air instead of smog, or if you don't mind commuting every day from the country to the city, then share the peaks and valleys of life with the Bernese Mountain Man!

Naughty Dog

You can't leave the Bernese Mountain Man alone for one second. He suffers from severe separation anxiety and can become very rebellious when he thinks he's being deserted, even to the point of throwing a tantrum and messing up the house as a cry for more attention!

New Trick

Teach the Bernese Mountain Man to socialize, get over his people phobia, and allow for new and different characters to join his inner kingdom. Otherwise the country air might get a bit too retiring, stifling, and claustrophobic for you!

Bichon Frise

Personality

Lights, camera, action! It's showtime as soon as you meet the Bichon Frise Man. His curious, playful, cute, and talkative demeanor will captivate you when you first meet him. This man is an artistic actor, brilliant producer, witty comic, or creative dancer who craves center stage. Performing and directing are in his blood and a natural pursuit for him. The Bichon Frise Man's ancestors were street performers for centuries throughout Europe and especially in France.

He's a friendly fellow, ready to entertain you, your friends, or a complete stranger at the drop of a hat. You can take him to any cultural event from a Broadway show to the local playhouse. His eyes will light up when he feels inspired and discovers new material to enhance his own repertoire. The only problem might be if the Bichon Frise Man gets too much in the moment—he might spontaneously jump up onstage uninvited and embarrass you. Successful Hollywood Bichon Frise Men are Martin Scorsese and Aaron Spelling.

If you find that this man matches your Juliet with his Romeo, and the two of you create the perfect love story—he's all yours! Mr. Bichon Frise is great with children, and he's the

kind of dad who won't mind dressing up as a clown on birthdays, or as Santa on Christmas. And you'll live happily entertained forever after.

Naughty Dog
The Bichon Frise Man's constant need to be in the limelight can be unnerving. His giant ego might need to be dropped off at the coat check every now and again. It might behoove him to let others have their fifteen minutes of fame.

New Trick
Yes, he's a dreamer, and living in the real world of responsibility might not be his strong suit. It's up to you to teach Mr. Bichon Frise that money is important to survive and can allow him a certain amount of creative freedom. If you have friends in the biz, introduce him to the art of networking.

Boston Terrier

Personality

Made in the USA! Mr. Boston Terrier is a dapper, homegrown fellow whose ancestors trace back to the early English settlers. He's an outgoing, extremely energetic blue blood. The Boston Terrier Man is an interesting mix of rugged American brawn and sweet gentleman. When you first meet him, he will show his receptive, well-mannered persona. Mr. Boston Terrier will be attentive and caring on your first romantic dinner date together. It's the party afterward that you should be concerned about! In a New York minute, the Boston Terrier Man can switch from Mr. Savoir Faire to Mr. Rock 'n' Roll party boy (no matter what his age). He possesses a wild side and loves to play all types of games, on and off the court. You're barking up the wrong tree if you can't keep up with the Boston Terrier Man's fast-paced lifestyle. He loves the city life!

His professional calling will find him in the position of entertainment producer, promoter, designer, restaurant entrepreneur, pilot, politician, real-estate developer, or any occupation where he can utilize all facets of his personality. All-American Boston Terrier President Teddy Roosevelt was an avid hunter, raised six children, and federally protected more

than 230 million acres of US soil! He was also the inspiration for the endearing term *teddy bear*! These sensitive men rock climb, ride motorcycles, fly planes, and take chances while still finding the time to adore and pamper the women in their lives. Life with the Boston Terrier Man is guaranteed to be a Boston tea party!

Naughty Dog

If the Boston Terrier Man sets his sights on you and you become the focus of his heart's desire—watch out! You might have to buy a watchdog to monitor his strong prey drive. All the attention might be flattering, but there's a fine line between being pursued and being consumed. Sometimes Mr. Boston Terrier crosses the line and needs to be firmly told: "Stay!"

New Trick

The Boston Terrier Man has an innate tendency to become distracted when his playful party side emerges. Three keywords that will help you center this man are *patience, consistency,* and *praise.* Demands don't work with him, but lots and lots of treats do!

Boxer

Personality

Do you know how to weave and bob like a prizefighter? You'll have to be in top form to stay in the ring with Mr. Boxer. The Boxer Man is a high-energy individual with a great deal of strength and stamina. You'll notice him immediately when he enters the room. The Boxer Man will amusingly approach his friends as if he's playfully going to box with them.

He's sporty and thrives on having an entertaining time whenever he can. Mr. Boxer's love of the good life can lead him to easy distraction and trouble if he isn't disciplined. He'll divertingly try to get your goat when you first start dating him. Don't let him get to you—don't play along! The Boxer Man is actually very sweet and sensitive after he gets to know a woman. And you won't be able to resist his cute little nose when he puts on the charm! Plan on having a large family if you start to hear wedding bells with Mr. Boxer. He's a demonstrative family man who adores children. Mr. Boxer expects to have a busy family life. If you marry this man, your weeks will consist of soccer games, flea markets, barbeques, movies, weekend trips, shopping, and many rounds of Scrabble and Monopoly. The Boxer Man will want you to keep up and

share the lead! You'll have to make sure he takes breaks within his eventful schedule; otherwise, he'll get overheated. Sylvester "Rocky" Stallone is a Boxer Man who couldn't be kept down! Legendary *Casablanca* Boxer Man Humphrey Bogart was known as a tough guy with a big heart. The Boxer Man might choose a career as a weight trainer, sports coach or agent, comedian, restaurant or club owner, athlete, entertainer, or deejay. He's a real knockout!

Naughty Dog

Mr. Boxer can tease you in front of his friends and get a big kick out of it, while you feel frustrated and publicly embarrassed. Don't let him get to you!

New Trick

The Boxer Man has to know you're in charge for him to respect and love you. You'll have to give him constant positive praise and lavish attention for him to react obediently. He secretly desires you to train him and keep him in line.

Bulldog

Personality

Ladies, step right up—introducing, in the Mr. Right corner, *Bulldog*! Bulldog Men come from a long line of British prizefighters. The Bulldog Man is much more tame than his ancestors, even to the point of being good-natured. Mr. Bulldog isn't the most handsome man on the block, but that won't matter once he cracks one of his famous jokes with his natural, goofy style. If humor turns you on, he's your man! He's one of the most down-to-earth guys you're going to meet. No pretensions here! If you are a stickler for good etiquette and social graces, this isn't the man for you. Mr. Bulldog devours his food, disregarding all manners, so beware until he's trained. Think: *Five-star restaurant? No. All-night diner? Yes!*

Mr. Bulldog tends to be attracted to the martial arts, the military, nightclub management, food catering, and athletic coaching. Bulldog Man Adam Sandler incorporates humor into most of his movies—*The Wedding Singer* and *Big Daddy*, for instance. Fred Durst of Limp Bizkit is the earthy, rock 'n' rolling Bulldog Man. And Jason Priestley is the racy Bulldog type.

You're going to need earplugs if you decide to spend the night, live with, or marry a Bulldog Man. Yes, this guy snores and sniffles while sleeping. When you wake up in the morning snarly and barking from yet another restless night, he'll do something silly, tell a joke, and make you laugh until you forget why you were upset in the first place. It's a part of Mr. Bulldog's undeniable charm.

Naughty Dog

Mr. Bulldog can become mouthy and snappy when he feels his territory is being threatened. He just can't control his macho response. His temperament originates genetically from a long line of ancestral warriors and fighters.

New Trick

The Bulldog Man tends to be immature and reactionary in his responses, but you can help him by gently pulling him aside and calmly explaining why such behavior at his age really isn't amusing or appropriate. Also, if you're planning to have a dinner party, offer him a much-needed class in Table Manners 101. If he goes along with the lesson, meet him halfway and promise a future food fight as his reward.

Chihuahua

Personality

Chicas, say "hola" to the land of the Chihuahua! This Latin lover's ancestry originates from Mexico and Central America and can be traced all the way back to the Aztec civilization. The modern Chihuahua Man can be very high-strung and nervous, especially in new social settings. It's important from the start that you introduce him to your close network of friends and family. Once he feels comfortable and warms up, he will delight everyone with entertaining and intellectual conversation. Mr. Chihuahua loves to be the center of attention. And don't let his small frame fool you: He's true to his Latino nature, strong and passionate.

A healthy outlet for his daily fire is a profession as a singer, dance instructor, publicist, radio personality, restaurant owner, news correspondent, or construction worker. Zealous and impassioned actor Mickey Rourke is a Chihuahua Man! His movies 9½ *Weeks* and *Angel Heart* display his ardent depth. Funny Chihuahua Man George Lopez's sitcom is based on his Latino roots!

Do I have to tell you what the perfect first date with a Chihuahua Man should be? That's right, put on the low-cut,

tight red dress, head off for a paella and sangria dinner, and cap the night with salsa dancing at a Latin dance club. He'll beam with pride as he sashays you center stage and claims the dance floor as his rightful territory. He'll become aggressive if another man tries to cut in on his turf. Save yourself the trouble and let him know he's the only man in the room for you. The Chihuahua Man will feel ten feet tall!

Naughty Dog
The Chihuahua Man can be very demanding and selfish if he doesn't get his own way. He possesses the nasty habit of sleeping anywhere in your apartment or house he chooses, including snoozing on your favorite antique sofa that took you two years to find!

New Trick
It's in your best interest not to baby the Chihuahua Man. His tendency is to become verbally aggressive when he thinks he's not getting enough attention. If you have to spend days away, distract him by renting Antonio Banderas movies, and leave him Carlos Santana CDs and several boxes of frozen Mexican food.

Chinese Crested

Personality

Two heads are better than one? Meet the Chinese Crested twins: Powderpuff and Hairless! As with most twins, these two men share common personality traits yet are very different. Both Chinese Crested brothers have an alert, intense expression and a highly playful, affectionate attitude toward life!

Do you want to nurture or be nurtured? Answering this question will help you choose which twin is for you. Ladies, here's the difference between these two men (it's fun to have choices). Powderpuff is the stronger, virile, outgoing, outdoorsy type, and prefers dining out and dancing all night to staying home. Hairless is the domestic, indoor man because of his sun-sensitive skin and weak constitution. He has to wear sunblock in the summer and an extra sweater in the winter, and prefers home-cooked meals and moonlit walks.

The Chinese Crested twins share more attributes: Both are friendly, devoted family men and treat friends and strangers like extended family members. For this reason they make great therapists, arbitrators, party planners, and

fund-raisers—professions in which they can bring people together. They're gifted climbers and jumpers, like the very agile Rayment twins, Neil and Adrian, from *The Matrix Reloaded.*

No matter which twin you choose, the other twin will always be in your life as a close family member. Ready? You're starring in your very own reality show. Drum roll, please . . . Which one will it be: Powderpuff or Hairless?

Naughty Dog

Chinese Crested Men can be too friendly for their own good and lack discretion when bringing home strangers. You might have to get used to every Tom, Dick, and Hairy (Harry) being invited to your home and social events.

New Trick

Chinese Crested Men are not the greatest protectors and judges of character. They naively think all breeds are simpatico. You might want to parlay some of your woman's intuition his way. He'll thank you when the other guy gets duped or conned instead of him.

Chow Chow

Personality

Knick-knack, paddywhack, give the Chow a bone! The Chow Chow Man's Chinese ancestors gave him his name, which translates to *knick-knack*. When you first meet the Chow Chow Man, you might think you've made a negative first impression because of the scowl on his face. Don't take it personally. He's just a very serious man with a reserved expression. Mr. Chow Chow treasures his independence and prefers the women he dates to keep him on a long leash. He'll snap at you if he thinks he's not free to roam when he wants. Give him some space; this man isn't a cheater. He's truly loyal and protective when in a committed relationship. And whatever you do, never sneak up on the Chow Chow Man from behind or beside him. He has poor eyesight and will get jumpy and startled. Try to approach him head-on at all times!

Probing thinker and psychologist Sigmund Freud was a Chow Man. Actor Ethan Hawke is a Chow Chow Man who chooses thought-provoking movie roles to reflect his talent. Chow Chow Man Walt Disney was quite inventive when he created his animated dynasty.

Mr. Chow Chow can live in the city or country as long as the temperatures are cool and the space is large. Say *ciao* to Mr. Chow if you're a woman who wants to have children. Most Chow Chow Men aren't especially playful or good with children. But if you're a professional woman who's decided against having children and opted for creating business ideas instead, he's the man! He'll choose a career as a farmer, cattle rancher, courier, security guard, waiter, mover, salesman, or postman. The Chow Chow Man is skeptical of strangers and will always shield you from suspicious types with one stern look!

Naughty Dog
Never remove the Chow Chow Man's meal from the table until he's completely finished. This man gets totally engrossed when he chows down. He'll get very irritable and might bite your hand off if his food is taken away or he doesn't get enough to eat. Please warn your waiter in advance when dining out!

New Trick
You'll have to teach the Chow Chow Man that he can relax with you. He's shy and doesn't like to be touched at first. Give him a massage and encourage him to let his guard down. Once he trusts you emotionally, he'll become more physically responsive.

Cocker Spaniel

Personality

Your Cocker Spaniel Man likes to hang out with the crowd but takes an unobtrusive stance. He's the kind of guy who will go out with his buddies and remain subtly in the background. Don't let him fool you, though; he's still an alert hunter at heart.

This cute, sweet, huggable man is active and high-strung. He's very sociable and befriends strangers. Don't expect him to become your guard dog. Mr. Cocker Spaniel can make you feel like you're the only woman in the room, while simultaneously checking out other females without you noticing. He just can't stop his mischievous curiosity and will be distracted at times. Mr. Cocker Spaniel will get snappy when you call him on his behavior. He responds more positively to intelligent conversation than to accusations. If you're a possessive woman in constant need of attention, Mr. Cocker Spaniel isn't the man for you. But if you're a confident woman who doesn't mind Cocker Spaniel Man's occasional flirting and inquisitiveness—then call this man home! Gently pull on his leash and lead him. He'll also respond positively to a teasing game of fetch. Once you do catch this man, you'll joyfully discover that he's great with children.

The Cocker Spaniel Man excels as a fashion designer, stylist, movie director, producer, entertainment agent, court judge, or actor. Actor Tom Selleck, a Cocker Spaniel Man, prefers to be in front of the camera!

Naughty Dog

Cocker Spaniel Man is too high-strung and distracted to clean up after himself. Yes, he's messy. You'll find dishes in the sink and dirty clothes in the corner. Out of the two of you, let's hope you don't mind being the more domestic one.

New Trick

To get Cocker Spaniel Man to bend to your desires, train him gently and calmly. He doesn't react well to abrupt demands or ultimatums. He's easily distracted and will escape by getting lost down a brand-new, unmarked trail.

Collie

Personality

Lassie, come home! The Collie Man is a great friend and companion to almost everyone he meets. He's friendly and very sociable, opening his world to every stranger on the corner, pizza deliveryman, and bank teller. He might even roam off with someone he met two minutes ago if he's in one of his restless moods!

The Collie Man doesn't like to be left alone for very long. You should address his constant feelings of abandonment if you don't want him to run off with a more sensitive gal. You might send him daily e-mails, call him often, and mail sweet greeting cards on a regular basis to help quell his insecurity. He has an insatiable desire to please, so let him know you love the way he pleases you, and tell him you appreciate his efforts. Mr. Collie prefers large living spaces and does his best if he has a big backyard, even in Gotham City.

This man has enormous marrying and fatherhood potential, although he tends to group his children and treat them as one large pack, not individuals. Collie Man Matthew Broderick plays many different acting roles, recently including proud father to a new pup.

Mr. Collie is such a congenial fellow that a profession as a missionary, diplomat, school counselor, performer, talk-show host, translator, negotiator, or politician is perfect for him. If you're the type of woman who enjoys socializing and meeting new people, then Mr. Collie can lead the welcome wagon to a blissful life of picnics, soirées, parties, and black-tie and other social events.

Naughty Dog
Mr. Collie can disappear in a flash! Smooth Collie Men are related to their Greyhound cousin, so they can be very, very fast, darting off and getting lost without a moment's notice. His restlessness can get the best of him, and roaming aimlessly might become a hobby for this sweet man.

New Trick
You might want to teach Mr. Collie that everyone he meets isn't a potential best friend and you wouldn't mind a little protection every now and then. Encourage him to enroll in a martial arts class or daily workouts; they'll help him harness his extra restless energy.

Dachshund

Personality

Have you heard the saying "Good things come in small packages"? That's what you can expect from Mr. Dachshund! He's the cute, small-framed man with the curious, playful look on his face. He's always waiting for a new adventure to take him away. With luck, you're the experience he's searching for! Don't let Mr. Dachshund's diminutive stature fool you; he's still a hunter at heart who loves a good challenge. If you combine this trait with his comedic, trickster side, you'll find a small bundle of fun surprises. The Dachshund Man thrives in both the countryside and the city. Talk to all the different sides of this man (and he does like to talk) by suggesting that you take a trip to Lake Tahoe for skiing and a comedy show. Next, plan to fly to San Francisco for a day of hunting for bargains, and a night of dancing and romancing.

Mr. Dachshund is family man too! He participates in all family activities and gets along great with children. Once you settle down with him you'll notice he practices a strange habit—he gets a kick out of digging! He won't mind weeding, planting trees, and landscaping your whole yard or maybe even the entire neighborhood! He makes a highly competent construction worker, landscaper, plumber, gardener, or cable or energy technician. Dachshund Man hockey star Wayne Gretsky dug his skates into ice for years! *Sopranos* Steve Schirripa is a Dachshund Man constantly burrowing his way out of trouble on the hit show. It's as if the Dachshund Man is digging to discover buried treasure, and you just might be the priceless jewel he's searching for!

Naughty Dog
What's the hullabaloo about? Mr. Dachshund can be a yapper and at times vocally snappish when he feels insecure. The Dachshund Man isn't above raising his voice and speaking over you during a heated discussion. Ladies, just remember: His bark is much worse than his bite.

New Trick
When the Dachshund Man gets in a mood, he can become antisocial and removed. He'll spend hours alone in his den, almost to the point of becoming a recluse. You need to teach him that everyone does need downtime, but not to the point of going underground!

Doberman Pinscher

Personality

Your Dober-Man is great marriage material. He loves having a sense of family, is a fine companion, and is good with children. This man gets a bad rap because of his well-known snappy temper. Hey, ladies, it stems from being possessive and protective of those he loves. What woman doesn't want to feel loved and have a strong shoulder to lean on now and again? Mr. Doberman's shielding arms create a safe haven to go home to after wrestling with the day-to-day jungle. You can curb a Pinscher (or should we say pincher) of his overpossessiveness by making him feel secure and a part of your social scene right from the start. He's very athletic, so joining a gym together would be a great way to channel all his extra high energy and a healthy way to bond with him. He's loyal, trustworthy, and affectionate when he feels safely placed in your life. If a Dober-Man has the slightest suspicions about your friends or other males in your surrounding territory, he will show his macho temper immediately and become antisocial as a show of protest. When out on the town with this man, don't play games or try to make him jealous—you might cause an embarrassing social situation.

Mr. Doberman makes an expert security specialist, fitness trainer, police officer, military man, private investigator, or homeland security agent. Celebrity trainer Dober-Man Radu guards his famous clientele's health and fitness! Actor Ashley Hamilton is a handsome, cavalier Dober-Man.

Naughty Dog

You have to make it clear right from the start that you will not put up with the Pinscher Man's notorious sarcasm and mouthy comments when he feels threatened. His territorial personality will make him become confrontational when he thinks another man might claim what is obviously and rightfully his. Tell him to muzzle it.

New Trick

You need to encourage Mr. Doberman's need for security at the beginning of your relationship. Try to balance quiet evenings at home and nights out on the town. When you're going to a party or a family gathering, immediately make him feel comfortable and part of the festivities. His friendly side will quickly surface. His bark is bigger than his bite!

German Sheperd

Personality

The German Shepherd Man is on a mission. He's the strong, stocky guy sitting in the corner of a party or club, scoping out the premises, waiting for something unusual to happen. Mr. German Shepherd is athletic, brave, and loyal—and one of the most intelligent breeds in town! He lives for solving a good mystery. Move over, David Caruso of *CSI: Miami*; there's a new supersleuth in town.

Mr. German Shepherd will choose a profession as an FBI or CIA agent, scientist, mathematician, investigative reporter, documentary filmmaker, or surgeon. German Shepherd piano man Elton John performs in flamboyant disguises and costumes!

Intrigue and mystery get the German Shepherd Man's juices flowing and turn him on. Create a secret suspense thriller of your very own. Keep him interested by keeping him guessing! Don't give up too much information about yourself, and don't always be available for him; otherwise, he'll be off trying to figure out another woman's riddle. Once you do have his curiosity piqued, plan the perfect evening out, full of unexpected twists and turns. Devise an amusing night of hide-and-seek! Tell Mr. German Shepherd to pick you up at

your apartment, and then leave before he arrives. Place a note on your front door with a clue leading him to your whereabouts. When he gets to the new destination, make it difficult for him to spot you. Sport a wig and sunglasses. Approach Mr. German Shepherd and introduce yourself using an accent and a fictitious name! He'll definitely play along! Life with this man will not be boring!

Naughty Dog

The German Shepherd Man can be incredibly cold and aloof when meeting strangers because of his suspicious mind. He's devoted and protective and doesn't like any other males infringing on his territory. This can be a problem when you try to expand your social circle.

New Trick

It will be your special mission to teach Mr. German Shepherd that it's important to learn to relax and enjoy life's simple pleasures. Teach him that life doesn't always have to be a remake of an Alfred Hitchcock movie. Simplifying his life is the missing clue!

Golden Retriever

Personality

Who's that soulful, sensitive, golden man sitting still in the corner? Welcome Mr. Golden Retriever into your life! Don't be hoodwinked by his low-key demeanor; he's a smooth operator. Once he spots you and finds you attractive, he will instantly approach and introduce himself. This man was born to hunt and retrieve! When the games begin, so does the fun! He's playful, spontaneous, and enthusiastic. Mr. Golden Retriever loves everything and everyone, including children, people, and other breeds.

He's an avid swimmer and will reside by the water. He'll enjoy work as a lifeguard, coast guardsman, resort manager, bartender, scuba diving instructor, or swimming coach. Many famous Golden Retriever Men who live by water and splash in the pools of success are Matt Lauer, Dave Price, Conan O'Brien, Steve Guttenberg, Enrique Iglesias, Ricky Martin, and Phil Donahue. The perfect romantic first date with Mr. Golden Retriever is dinner at a restaurant overlooking the water, followed by a sizzling night of dancing at a happening club.

If you're not sure about making a commitment with the Golden Retriever Man, it's better to take this relationship

slowly! The word *no* isn't in his vocabulary. The Golden Retriever Man will use his lovable qualities to get what he wants when he wants it and how he wants it. When he looks at you with those playful eyes, don't melt into submission! Otherwise, you'll have one adorable but spoiled puppy on your hands!

Naughty Dog

What's yours is his! Golden Retriever Man is not above going through your closets and personal belongings when you're not looking. He feels entitled to your possessions. He won't think twice about wearing your sweaters, jeans, or jackets—let's just hope he steers clear of your dresses and pumps!

New Trick

Help Mr. Golden Retriever channel his high energy by giving him projects to do around the house or yard. When you suggest that he become your handyman, do so with a healthy dose of compassion. He can become subservient if he thinks you're being too harsh with him. And there's nothing sadder than seeing this man walk away with his tail between his legs.

Great Dane

Personality

Who's that godly creature who just walked into the room? Enter Mr. Great Dane. Yes, he's head and shoulders above the rest. His majestic presence and kingly gait make him impossible to miss. Don't let this gentle giant intimidate you, though. He's a sensitive and easygoing man. Mr. Deutsche Dogge (his background is German) is aware of his immense size and never uses his strength to wield his power over lesser mortals. He'll unleash his enormous strength only when pitted against the most formidable foe. The Great Dane Man doesn't mind being noticed, because he's social and friendly by nature. You can take him almost anywhere, but I do suggest you avoid small, crowded bars or rooms. He needs lots of legroom and just won't feel comfortable if he's cramped!

When buying Mr. Great Dane a birthday or holiday sweater, remember that he's a very large man. Hmmm, makes you wonder, doesn't it, ladies? The perfect profession for this man is basketball player, public speaker, military man, politician, long-distance runner, engineer, or mechanic. *Ace Ventura* Great Dane Jim Carrey plays a hilarious slapstick pet detective!

Mr. Great Dane is a well-mannered gentlemen and a fine companion. He's marriage material and is *great* with children. This man is just a big softy at heart.

Naughty Dog

If you don't have a very large apartment or home, Mr. Big might become a liability. When he arrives at the party you're having with the live rock band, set aside a special section for him on the dance floor. Otherwise he might try to impress you with some creative moves, end up destroying some of your prize possessions, and accidentally knock out your best friend.

New Trick

It's important that Mr. Great Dane spends an equal amount of time indoors and outdoors. You can help him balance his enormous strength by scheduling long, romantic moonlit walks and then leading him back to your (let's hope) sizable humble abode.

Greyhound

Personality

Fast, faster, fastest! This man is built for speed. Have you signed up for aerobic classes yet? If you want to keep up with the Greyhound Man, you'd better make sure that your cardiovascular system is in tip-top shape. He's used to hanging with the jet set, and his ancestors were known for running with the aristocratic British nobility during the 1800s. Although he prefers the fast lane, this sleek, long-legged hunk can be reserved, quiet, and timid at times.

Mr. Greyhound is fiercely independent. If he suddenly, secretly disappears, you can bet your money on one sure thing: He can be found at the racetrack. He's sporty by nature and gets a thrill from gambling on everything, from the Indianapolis 500, Kentucky Derby, Super Bowl, World Series, and Olympics to the local boccie-ball tournament. The odds are in your favor if you plan to take Mr. Greyhound on a surprise jaunt to Las Vegas, Atlantic City, or, if your purse allows it, enchanting Monte Carlo. He loves his creature comforts. Make sure your hotel suite is fully equipped with all his favorite amenities, including that sexy evening wear you want to try out on him. Chances are if you roll the dice with this eager-to-please man,

you'll end up a winner! *Alien* star Sigourney Weaver happily took a gamble with her Greyhound husband, Jim Simpson, artistic director and founder of Manhattan's Flea Theater.

Mr. Greyhound might be a professional race-car driver, jockey, horse breeder and trainer, speed ice-skater, Wall Street day trader, or pilot.

Naughty Dog

Although Mr. Greyhound likes high-speed situations and toys, he also has a reputation for being quite the couch potato. One minute he's Superman, moving faster than a speeding bullet . . . and the next minute a bullet aimed at him wouldn't get him off the couch!

New Trick

The Greyhound Man is a sprinter! He might not be able to go the distance, though, as he burns out quickly. You must teach him to steady his energy and educate him on endurance. Stamina is important, isn't it, ladies?

Irish Setter

Personality

Oh, Danny Boy! Mr. Irish Setter is the good-looking Irishman with rich chestnut red hair. He's the strong, sturdy, and elegant man hanging out with his social pack. He has an enormous amount of energy, and when he's out with his friends it's like a modern-day version of *Gangs of New York*! His motto is "The more the merrier!" He's extremely good-natured and enthusiastic when he finds something or someone he wants to hunt. Pray that you're his prey!

On your first date, suggest an Irish pub that serves authentic Irish dishes such as shepherd's pie, fish and chips, and beef stew. It sounds cliché, but have you ever met an Irishman who doesn't like potatoes? You're in for a social late night, with lots of laughs, singing, and carousing. He has the stamina of ten men and will perform a special jig just for you when you're home alone together.

If you get serious with Mr. Irish Setter Man, you should know that he's a loyal, affectionate family man. He'll want to have offspring but does better with small children; he doesn't have the patience for babies. The Irish Setter Man is financially responsible but will choose a career that will provide a healthy outlet for all his vim and vigor. He might be a fireman, restaurant and pub owner, policeman, athlete, military man, construction worker, performer, politician, or physician.

With the Irish Setter Man, you have found not only a pot of gold at the end of the rainbow, but also a heart of gold. When asked what dog encapsulates the characteristics of his ideal woman, *Saved by the Bell* and *The Other Half* costar Mario Lopez said, "The Irish Setter. They are sleek with shiny red hair. I have a thing for redheads!"

Naughty Dog

When this breed is naughty, he's very naughty! Mr. Irish Setter can party all night with his buddies and not think twice about the time—or you! So don't expect him to call you exactly when the clock strikes twelve. He gets a kick out of running with the wolves!

New Trick

Subtly explain to Mr. Irish Setter that if he wants to have those namesake pups he's already bragging about, he's going to have to settle down a bit. Help him realize that the four-leafed clover he's searching for can be found in your garden, not the pub!

Labrador Retriever

Personality

Who's the tanned Adonis in his Speedo, walking on the beach and playing Frisbee? Say hello to the Labrador Retriever Man. He's an energetic, active, and social man who loves the good life! If he's the object of your desire, get to the gym, and don't forget your bikini waxing! You're going to be spending most of your time at the beach. The Lab Man will either live or work by the water. Plan an evening by making reservations on a private boat for dinner. Later, take a romantic dip in a moonlit ocean, swimming pool, or Jacuzzi. You're sure to make a big splash with him! The Labrador Retriever Man finds success as a politician, actor, athlete, entrepreneur, architect, or interior designer, with an office that overlooks the water.

Lab Man former president Bill Clinton often eats at the Black Dog restaurant while vacationing on Martha's Vineyard. Lab rocker Keith Richards was instrumental in writing the Rolling Stones' hit song "Beast of Burden." Actor Lab Man Rupert Everett played a major role in his *Best Friend's Wedding*.

You should know that Lab Men have duck fetishes. They can identify with ducks because of a shared love of water. You'll

find an interior duck motif throughout Mr. Labrador Retriever's home. The perfect gag gift for him, of course, is a rubber ducky for his bathtub!

The Lab Man thrives when praised and appreciated. The more you give, the more you'll get with this man! Lucky you—he likes to please. Don't worry, though; if you hook up with Mr. Labrador Retriever, you won't get waterlogged. He welcomes a calm home life on land, grounded with children and other animals too!

Naughty Dog

The Lab Man can be mischievous; he can also stray and find trouble if he gets bored. It's up to you to keep him mentally stimulated and interested. If you succeed, you'll be the single female body of water he dives in to. Splish-splash!

New Trick

Mr. Labrador Retriever spends lots of his free time at the beach and often forgets to wear sunblock. It's imperative that you drive home the importance of skin protection and the damage the sun's rays can do to his sensitive skin. He'll thank you twenty years from now.

Maltese

Personality

Mr. Maltese is the guy who gets away with everything! Why? Because he can! His regal disposition and downright good looks allow him to charm his way in or out of any situation he chooses. The Maltese Man can mingle with the upper echelon of society without question. He's been known to have lunch with construction workers and dinner with kings.

If your version of Mr. Right is a man who is capable of being your best friend and companion, look no farther. He can proudly walk you, arm in arm, into any red-carpet social event. Once the party begins, you'll be surprised at how he's on a first-name basis with most of the guests. Prince Maltese possesses such a lovable and playful disposition that everyone rallies to his side for a good time. His Highness thrives on all the extra attention! He'll verbally let you know when he feels unappreciated. And he's great with children, because he's so childlike himself!

Stylist extraordinaire and Maltese Man Steven Cojacaru of *Entertainment Tonight* is viewed by thousands of loyal fans weekly. Maltese Man guitarist Richie Sambora of Bon Jovi dated Cher and many other leading ladies before he married

Heather Locklear. The perfect profession for Mr. Maltese is an antiques dealer, party planner, real-estate mogul, movie producer, painter, art collector, or dealer.

So, ladies, if you like to hold court, be seen in all the right places, and socialize till the wee hours, Maltese Man is the right pooch for you.

Naughty Dog

Mr. Maltese is the prince of his domain and feels entitled to do whatever he wants. The Maltese Man is popular and spoiled by his family and friends. This can cause him to become undisciplined and difficult to live with—or date—because he doesn't keep to a schedule very well.

New Trick

Do yourself a favor and don't indulge every one of Mr. Maltese's whims. It's important to lay down the law and set boundaries and time limitations from the beginning of your relationship. Otherwise, this relationship might become a free-for-all. Stop the yapping and the fur from flying before it starts!

Mutt

Personality

The Mutt Man is a worldly Renaissance man! He's a smart, smooth operator, a lovable homebody, and an athlete with a curious mind, individually or all wrapped up in one body. His background is a potpourri of different nationalities and genetic influences. You might think you're dating Mr. Labrador Retriever when suddenly, while you're at the beach swimming, he becomes Mr. Greyhound and wants to dry off and head for the horse races to place a bet on a sure thing. Or, just when you're sitting down to have dinner and engage in stimulating conversation with Mr. Poodle, he does an about-face and starts singing show tunes with the piano player. Yes, he's part Bichon Frise Man! You're going to have to remain agile, flexible, and spontaneous to keep up with the Mutt Man's changing moods. You'll never be bored with Mr. Mutt, because he's always unleashing a different side of his complex makeup. He has a natural humanitarian side, and he can compassionately identify with diverse groups of people from different walks of life.

Mr. Mutt will choose a career in the entertainment industry, medical field, international exporting business, not-for-profit organization, or any profession that allows him to utilize the

many facets of his personality. Famous multitalented Mutt Man actors are sexy Brad Pitt of *Thelma and Louise*, mysterious David Duchovny of *The X-Files*, and animated Alan Cumming of *X2: X-Men United*.

Buy a computer program that helps trace your Mutt Man's family tree. Invite him over for dinner and later help him discover his roots. Maybe you'll find that your ancestors and Mr. Mutt's lived in the same small region of a different continent hundreds of years ago.

Naughty Dog

Mr. Mutt can feel scattered and ungrounded at times, causing him to make hasty decisions without thinking about the consequences. His insecurities can affect his ability to open up and become vulnerable with you.

New Trick

Teach the Mutt Man that his multifaceted background makes him interesting and exciting. Encourage him to celebrate his uniqueness and share his experience with you and the world!

Pomeranian

Personality

Abracadabra from Iceland! You've just met Mr. Pomeranian, and immediately you're charmed off your feet. This man is a foxy spell weaver, and you'll find yourself in a love trance after the first dance. He's not a tall man, but so cocky and self-confident that you won't notice. Mr. Pomeranian is a bundle of energy and thrives on being busy and working a full day.

One warning when you're dealing with Pomeranian Man! This Houdini is intelligently alert and isn't above using tricky manipulation to get you to bow to his desires. It will be difficult to break the hold he has over you—not that you'll want him to! So what if the Pomeranian Man is a little mischievous? Bad boys can be sexy. A perfect example is Pomeranian Man Ozzy Osbourne, known for his outrageous live performances and hit MTV reality show!

Don't expect long, cozy nights in front of the fireplace with this man. He's playful and always ready for the next great adventure, but he's not very affectionate. You might get invited to go skydiving, scuba diving, bungee jumping, skateboarding, speedboating—you get the idea. He loves living on the edge. Obviously he would make the perfect magician, lawyer,

arbitrator, traveling salesman, stockbroker, business consultant, or advertising salesman—any profession in which he can use his talented verbal skills and charm to prove a point or close the deal.

Ladies, we all could use a little more magic in our lives, and that's what you'll find with this hypnotic man.

Naughty Dog

Now you see him—now you don't! The Pomeranian Man's shenanigans can get tiresome. He can be perceived as a troublemaker. His playful antics might be totally misunderstood by others. Tell his critics it's all in fun!

New Trick

The Pomeranian Man's constant need for adventure might have him bouncing off the walls of your home like a jumping bean. Housebreaking will be an ongoing labor of love. Teach him that staying home alone with you can be the ultimate trip.

Poodle

Personality

Do you have a master's degree from Harvard or Yale? Are you well versed in many conversational subjects? You'd better be if you have your eye on the Poodle Man. The second he walks in the room, you can't help but notice this intelligent and impeccably well-dressed man. He wears designer duds and grooms himself from head to toe. He's the pedigree with a pedicure. If you're brave enough to approach Mr. Poodle first, he'll be impressed by your confidence. Your opening line should be a witty question. Then prepare for clever repartee (and possibly sparks) to fly between you. Mr. Poodle Mensa Man isn't above using his high IQ to outsmart you and get his own way.

The Poodle Man is an exciting date because he's not only a thinker; he's also energetic and spirited! *Titanic* Poodle Man Leonardo DiCaprio is spotted jet-setting all around the globe! Poodle politician Winston Churchill was renowned for his brilliant speeches during World War II. The Poodle Man makes an excellent professor, writer, scientist, publisher, orchestra conductor, corporate CEO, or clothes designer.

When you're planning an outing, give Poodle Man a long list of options to choose from. Suggest going to the circus,

opera, foreign movie, jazz club, Smithsonian, or Caribbean! He'll enjoy toying with and discussing each idea in depth with you before deciding on a final destination. You'll keep the Poodle Man interested by keeping him intellectually stimulated. By the way, if he does choose the trip to the Caribbean, pack your bikini—the Poodle is a natural-born swimmer.

Naughty Dog

Mr. Poodle is the absentminded professor type! While you're in the middle of a stimulating conversation with him, he'll jump up and run to his desk to jot down yet another new idea. When he finally gets around to cooking you that gourmet meal he promised, he'll suddenly remember the call to his business partner. Thirty minutes later, his special béarnaise sauce is burned and he orders a pizza instead.

New Trick

Mr. Poodle instigates intellectual contests of wills when he's bored and unfocused. If he gets involved in a disciplined competitive sport, he'll become less argumentative and scattered. He responds very well to praise. Such a good Poodle Man!

Pug

Personality

Give Mr. Pug a welcome hug! Pug Man is the funny-looking man with big, bold, expressive eyes. And yes, he could use some moisturizer on those wrinkles and laugh lines. Blame his ancestors for his wrinkles! They moved from ancient China to Europe and finally to the United States. It's exhausting just thinking about it! Mr. Pug is a diminutive man, but still confident and playful and a dignified companion. By far his most distinctive attribute is his witty sense of humor. Laughter is a well-known aphrodisiac, and Mr. Pug will have you turned on with a smile. He's a show-off and has a reputation for cavorting around town. Don't let this intimidate you; instead, get dressed to the nines and join him!

Are you worried that the Pug Man isn't serious enough to settle down and make a firm commitment? He is highly affectionate, likes to please, and is a true best friend and family man. When you do get to house hunting together, choose a city or town with cooler climates, such as Seattle or San Francisco. He doesn't do well in the heat.

The Pug Man's chosen profession might be comedy writer, comedian, school or camp counselor, restaurant maître d',

teacher, or personnel executive. He excels in occupations in which social skills, leadership, and levity are required. *Cheers* to funny sitcom Pug Men Ted Danson and Woody Harrelson for comically entertaining audiences for more than a decade! Mr. Pug will have you laughing all the way to the altar.

Naughty Dog

Although Mr. Pug is a sweetie at heart, he does have a very stubborn streak. He can be quite obstinate and mouthy when opposed. Sometimes he possesses the awkward foot-in-mouth syndrome. The Pug Man can crack a joke at exactly the wrong time.

New Trick

The Pug Man's always on the go and can get so distracted that he forgets to put his shoes on before he walks out the front door. Show him that repetition and a balanced schedule will keep his life more organized.

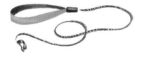

Rottweiler

Personality

Hail, Caesar! Mr. Rottweiler is a Roman gladiator at heart. His Italian roots travel back to the days of Roman troop marches to victory. Today you might find the Rottweiler Man sporting a security guard uniform, secret service shades, or military boots.

Rottweiler Man Will Smith wore dark shades in *Men in Black* and shot it out with the bad guys in *Wild Wild West*. He's also known in Hollywood as being very protective of his wife, Jada, and their children. The Rottweiler Man's natural instinct is to guard any territory he feels responsible for, whether it's his country, bank account, or family. If all goes as planned, he'll want to shelter you too! He's very confident and can make a snap decision when it's needed.

Mr. Rottweiler is self-assured, smart, courageous, and domineering. If you'd like to find a way to bond with this man, go straight for his heart. Enroll both of you in a weekend afternoon karate or fencing class. Then it's off to an epic war movie, and cap the night with a plate of pasta and bottle of vino at a cozy corner Italian restaurant. He'll be crooning your praises! When he mentions that he wants to bring you home to meet Mama—make sure you go! The Rottweiler Man wants to

marry, have children, and carry on his family name, but not before he gets his mother's approval. He's a traditional family man and herds his relatives together whenever he can. Holidays are a special and joyous time with Mr. Rottweiler!

Naughty Dog

The Rottweiler Man can be as bossy as the Godfather. His desire to protect can become overly compulsive and obsessive when he's dealing with those he loves. Highly wary of strangers, he's not above using one of his many connections to check out your long-lost friend who suddenly reappears on your front doorstep.

New Trick

You'll need the patience of an angel when trying to quell Mr. Rottweiler's suspicious mind. This isn't a small task and will take tolerance and perseverance on your part. Your best approach will be to introduce him to new people and social settings in recurring dates. Once he feels comfortable, he'll surprise you by keeping it loose.

Saint Bernard

Personality

Do you want to be rescued by love? Then Mr. St. Bernard is the man to find and save you. This tall, patient, and calm man might not be the life of the party, but he is one of the most responsible gentlemen around. If you bark up his family tree, you'll discover that his roots started back in Switzerland, and his relatives were known for search-and-rescue missions throughout the region. So, Swiss Miss, get your best yodeling voice in shape and call this man home.

St. Bernard Man is likely to be working with the Coast Guard or various search-party groups, as a fireman, lifeguard, paramedic, private investigator, or FBI agent, or in any vocation in which he can use his natural instincts to locate the injured and missing. Charles Grodin plays a dependable St. Bernard Man in the animal-friendly *Beethoven* movies. Mr. St. Bernard's stature might be deceiving; he looks too large to move for long periods of time. He has a great deal of stamina, though, is dependable in emergency situations, and provides a certain level of security. This savior of a man can be your very own Rock of Gibraltar.

A fun, recreational date would be to create your own seek-and-find drill. Take him to a mountainside, local park, crowded beach, or packed dance club. Tell him you're going for a short walk alone and if you're not back in ten minutes, he should find you. Don't return, but do leave clues along the way: your scarf wrapped around a tree, a message in the sand, a note on a napkin delivered by a waiter. While he's searching for you, sneak up behind him! Later, reward your St. Bernard Man for being such a good sport with a hot cup of cocoa—or something much sweeter.

Naughty Dog

St. Bernard Man isn't always a saint! He can be very stubborn and he moves at his own pace. You might feel you have to hire a bulldozer to get him off the couch or floor. He won't budge when he doesn't want to. And what's with the drooling, already!

New Trick

It might seem as if you have to set off fireworks around Mr. St. Bernard to get him excited about anything that isn't a life-or-death situation. He's a fine solo companion, but introduce him to the idea that life can be a bowl of cherries and great fun when he socializes with others more often.

Shih Tzu

Personality

Shih Tzu (whose name translates to *lion dog*) is the original Zen man. His ancesters originated in Tibet, and he comes from a long line of Buddhists. Ancient Chinese royalty took a special liking to his ancestors.

The Shih Tzu Man is the upbeat, sweet, thin but toned, wiry guy with the long, beautiful mane of hair (but not more luxurious than yours). Don't let his small frame fool you; he has a lot of energy and can be quite tough if the situation requires him to be. This man requires a healthy dose of daily exercise. The Shih Tzu Man might choose a career as a performer, yoga instructor, philosophy professor, hairdresser, spiritual adviser, or astrologer. Legendary crooner Frank Sinatra was a Shih Tzu Man. He howled and hunted with his very own Rat Pack! Shih Tzu boy band Hanson sang and chanted "MMM Bop" all the way to the top of the pop charts! And Shih Tzu billionaire Bill Gates created a computer worldwide change of consciousness with Microsoft.

When you start dating Mr. Shih Tzu, sign the two of you up for yoga classes at the local center or ashram. After class, it's back to your temple of love. Light some incense, dim the lights,

play ethereal new-age music, order Chinese takeout, and watch this man become your gentle lapdog. Hey, if you help him balance his chi, Shih Tzu Man might propose on one knee. Yes, he's marriage material and good with children. If you do decide that Mr. Shih Tzu is the one, your morning mantra should be: *Ohmmm . . . Shih Tzu Man, commitment is at hand.*

Naughty Dog

Shih Tzu Man does have a prominent stubborn streak that he hides behind his playful nature. When a point of contention arises between the two of you, he might not budge an inch. Teach him the ancient art of compromise. He'll reach his much-sought-after nirvana!

New Trick

Mr. Shih Tzu prefers to keep his lion's-mane hair long. Sometimes he wears a ponytail. He might start to look like a madman or wacky professor if he doesn't properly take care of his hair. The next time you go shopping for shampoo and conditioner, pick up some hair products for your Shih Tzu Man, and introduce him to the world of hair care.

Siberian Husky

Personality

Mush! That's what will happen to your heart the second you meet Mr. Siberian Husky. He's the handsome Russian hunk with the gorgeous blue or brown eyes. And they don't call him husky for nothing! He's strong, powerful, and fast, and he has great endurance. The Siberian Husky Man's character is a sturdy combination of clever wit, mischievous adventure, and stubborn independence.

Your dating progress with the Siberian Husky Man will move along quicker if you sincerely like his closest friend. His friend is going to be a big part of the overall picture! These two fun-loving buddies do practically everything together. They can spend hours discussing a gamut of subjects from Olympic competitions, government conspiracy plots, and the newest styles of jeans to their next skiing excursion. At least the conversations won't get boring!

Mr. Siberian Husky performs better in cooler temperatures and prefers to live closer to the Canadian border than south of the border. If you do settle down and have little Eskimos with this man, your winter months will be full of fun games and sports. The Siberian Husky Man has a preference for outdoor professions such as a snow plow operator, ski instructor, military transport engineer, landscaper, construction worker, long-distance runner, excavator, or sled racer. This man promises to pull you through the different terrains of commitment with effortless ease, fun adventure, and loving affection. *Zoolander* funnyman Ben Stiller is a Husky Man who pulls his weight with laughter! Husky Man joker Tom Green goes the distance in *Road Trip*.

Naughty Dog

The late-night carousing and clever capers that Mr. Siberian Husky and his best friend are always planning can get quite tiresome when you want some quiet time alone with this man. He's not above barking loudly when opposed!

New Trick

The trick here is to teach him a trick. The Siberian Husky Man resists change, and modifying any of his behaviors is going to take patience on your part. Offer him as many treats as possible without spoiling him!

West Highland Terrier

Personality

Do you hear the faint sound of Scottish bagpipes approaching? That's Mr. West Highland Terrier entering your life. You'll recognize him immediately! He's the guy with the great teeth and friendly smile. Don't worry about making the first move. He's curious and independent enough to approach you without hesitation. The West Highland Terrier Man has the gift of gab and makes everyone he meets feel comfortable right from the start, including you! Once the preliminaries are over, don't be surprised when he invites you to an outing. This man loves the great outdoors. Go out and buy that kayaking, mountain-climbing, and bicycle gear if you plan on dating him seriously. The worst that can happen is you'll get in great shape—and he won't mind when your tummy gets toned.

Mr. West Highland Terrier is affectionately demonstrative, albeit demanding. He'll expect you to keep up with his full itinerary. He has an insatiable hunger for being in the know and in the middle of what's happening. For this reason, he's a natural politician, news or sports reporter, commentator, actor, journalist, professor, teacher, or public relations executive.

Designer West Highland Terrier Man Tommy Hilfiger fits this profile, as his clothing designs are seen on many celebs and their dogs! If Mr. West Highland Terrier's schedule is too busy for you—then head east. But if you do, you'll miss out on answering an age-old mysterious question: Exactly what is underneath that kilt?

Naughty Dog

The West Highland Terrier Man is highly sociable and doesn't like to make waves. Diplomacy is his middle name, and he believes in letting bybones be bybones—whoops—bygones be bygones. Although he's very loyal, don't expect him to fight your battles for you. He prefers to keep the atmosphere light and avoids heated confrontations.

New Trick

What's the rush? Between Mr. West Highland Terrier's outdoor activities and his social calendar—when will you ever find quality time alone together? You'll have to teach him that your private time can be as exciting and fulfilling as the next grand opening. Fads fade, but true love lasts!

Yorkshire Terrier

Personality

Mr. Yorkshire Terrier is that cutie in the window, the one with the waggly tail! He's the guy with that irresistible, inquisitive face that draws you closer with each look. Don't let his small stature trick you; he's a fearless man with a propensity for trouble and adventure. Mr. Yorkie isn't above starting quarrels with anyone that opposes his opinions; he gets a rise out of verbal sparring matches, even with a complete stranger. That's what makes him the quintessential lawyer, arbitrator, business manager, or agent. Ladies, his adorable, impeccable looks, British wit, and energized spirit convince everyone that he's the man of the hour and should be listened to. The Yorkshire Terrier Man is a big man in a small body, and that goes double for his ego! If he's charmed you, he'll let you know from the start that he's the boss, whether you're out on the town or at home. He's so lovable that you'll probably give in to his demands; just hope for your own sake that they're within reason.

Mr. Yorkie is usually not the outdoor type and prefers indoor activities. Yorkie Man quarterback Brett Favre of the Green Bay Packers is an exception. He's known for being a calculating, tough player on the field and a big, playful kid at heart off of it!

The average Yorkie Man partakes in short bouts of exercise but favors mental gymnastics and marathons. Expect him to have at least fifty explanations for why working out is overrated and unnecessary. Your rebuttal? Tell your Yorkie Man that you expect him to keep up when court recesses and the two of you create a sexy, private, world-class-action suite at home.

Naughty Dog

The Yorkshire Terrier Man does like his creature comforts and would rather stay home when he has free time. The problem here is that he turns the household upside down and makes a huge mess. He doesn't mind suddenly falling asleep in the middle of his dirty clutter.

New Trick

Mr. Yorkie can have a slight Napoleon complex, causing him to compensate for his size by talking back and being bossy. You'll have to build and soothe his sensitive ego, convincing him that he's perfect as is, and that's why you love him so!

CHAPTER THREE

Training Tips

"Here, gentlemen, a dog teaches us a lesson in humanity."

NAPOLEON BONAPARTE

"M*en are dogs!*" Many different women dating a gamut of breeds (and mutts) of men have howled this for many different reasons. This chapter will provide you with a guideline of specific humorous training tips and canine commands to follow if you want to be more in control of your relationship. Remember, ladies, the first two months are critical when disciplining your man, and from day one it's up to you to set the tone for the whole relationship. Don't be shy, shorten that leash, give your commands when he's being a naughty puppy, and take charge if you think this man is the one!

Have you ever wanted to tell your man "No" and didn't know how to do it without upsetting or offending him? I'll enlighten you on how and when it's the appropriate time to use this canine command and other commands such as Come, Sit, Stay, Down, and Roll Over. You'll enjoy trying the commands on your man and finding exactly the correct one to use for each new situation when necessary. Your breed might not understand what's happening at first, but before he knows it he'll be out of the doghouse and happily in your arms. That's the perfect time to bestow on him the unique treats that only you can supply and that he finally deserves.

Housebreaking a man can be one of the most difficult tasks a woman can undertake when she decides to marry or cohabitate. I provide an instructive training tip on how to accomplish this task with ease and levity. Before long, your man will be scratching and barking at the front door to get in—not out! Does your preferred man have a barking problem when he doesn't get his way? I will help you conquer this problem and any jealousy he might display when feeling insecure by different training techniques, including one that is sure to become his favorite training tip: touching!

This chapter provides hands-on training advice that will be pleasurable to execute and will place you in control of your relationship while creating a deeper and more trusting emotional bond with the man in your life.

No

How many times have you wanted to say something to your man when you were unhappy with his behavior, but you remained muzzled because you didn't want to upset or lose him? One-word commands are very critical when setting the rules and boundaries of your relationship from the first meeting. Both men and dogs have a difficult time hearing the word No at first, but it will become the most important command you can teach your man. Let's say you made reservations to have dinner with him, and the night you're expecting to rendezvous, his best friend calls with two tickets to some event he just has to go to. At the last minute he asks whether he can cancel with you. It's up to you to set the standards! Look firmly into his eyes when

he's in one of his selfish moods, and sternly tell him "No." Let him know that you mean no, and don't back down no matter what excuse he's concocted. Consistency is the key to making this command work. It's also important to use this command wisely; otherwise, your man won't take you seriously and will laugh–or bark—it off.

Come

The second-most-useful command is
Come. Men and dogs are similar; they
both explore new territories and stray
whenever their curiosity gets the best of
them. And they respond eagerly and
equally to the command Come because
they think they will be getting affection
and attention from you. You must use
this command every time you sense your
man is losing interest, even if it means
keeping him on a short leash outdoors

and indoors. When you're walking through the park with your
man, don't be alarmed if suddenly he spots a beautiful woman on
Rollerblades in short-shorts. Instead, gently place your arm in his,
and whisper in his ear that you have a special lingerie treat back
at your place you want to try on for him. Teach your man to relate
to the command Come with pleasure and treats. Don't use it to
punish him, or he'll take off running the first chance he gets!

Sit

Men and dogs have short attention spans and difficulty sitting
still for long periods of time. Blame it on their natural instinct
to play games and hunt! When your man is constantly sniffing

around and driving you crazy with his unending distractions, it's time to use the Sit command. Encourage your man to sit by leading him to a chair, couch, or park bench, and sitting first. Then take his hand and guide him next to you while gently saying the word Sit. This training tip is exceptionally useful if you're out with friends or family at a restaurant and your husband, boyfriend, or date gets up right in the middle of dinner and disappears. When you finally find him talking to the bartender and watching a sporting event, escort him back to the table and say, "Sit." If he gets up again (which is probable if a game is on), continue practicing the Sit command until he remains seated long enough for you to praise him and give him a nuzzle or a kiss on the cheek. This command works well with

the Stay command: "Sit . . . stay." Eventually he will get it and sit long enough for everyone to finish dinner, including him! The Sit command is also helpful when you drag him to a romantic movie, on a clothes-shopping excursion, to a wedding, or to the ballet!

Stay

When it comes to men and dogs, they either stay or stray. It's up to you to show your man that it's more advantageous for him to stay than go. The Stay command will prevent your man from running out the front door every time it opens, discourage him from flirting with the new office hottie, and make him think twice when other dogs call him out to run with the wolves every night. The Stay command works especially well coupled with the No command. As with all the training tips, consistency from the start will produce positive results. Let's say your man is over for a romantic evening and his cell phone rings. He answers and gets a last-minute invitation to join the wild pack at a club opening. He asks whether it would be all right if he leaves and catches up with you later. Not what you intended to happen, right? Tell him firmly, "No, it's not okay," and then affectionately, sweetly, and seductively say, "Stay." Nine times out of ten, he will rethink his options and decide to hang out with you. If this command doesn't work the first time you say "Stay," try using his name the second time, for example, "Stay, Peter." You'll have the confirming pleasure of watching him melt and turn off his cell phone!

Down

Have you ever had one of those nights when you spend two hours primping and getting dressed to perfection (or as close as possible), and just as you're ready to walk out the door, your main squeeze gets in one of his feisty moods and starts to jump all over you? If so, here's the training tip for you! Just say "Down!" This is one of the most difficult commands to teach both men and dogs because they live in the moment and tend to get carried away when wanting to play. The Down command will require a great deal of time and patience on your part, but the results will be well worth your effort. Another situation in which the Down command is appropriate is when you're having a cocktail party and your husband, boyfriend, or date won't leave your guests alone. He has a potential client cornered and is chewing his or her ear off. Walk over, gently pull your beau away, and sweetly say, "Down." Again, this command requires repetition to take effect. Don't be surprised if you have to use the Down training tip on your man several times on the same night before it finally sinks in!

Roll Over

There's nothing more amusing than watching a dog having a
playful time and rolling over on command. The Roll Over
command is especially useful when you want your man to jump
off the couch that's he's been lounging on all day to play with
you. He won't mind when you incorporate some recreational
tickling, touching, and carousing. Say "Roll over" when
he keeps you up all night snoring like a bear. Since he
subconsciously associates "Roll over" with fun, he'll instantly
move over or go belly up while sleeping. Men and dogs both
like affectionate touching and having their bellies rubbed.
After a good meal, most men will automatically rub their own
stomachs when joyfully satiated!

Trick or Treats

Men and dogs love their treats! Both get elated and excited
about a new toy, refuse to share it, and tend to destroy it. The
trick to bestowing treats is to reward your man only when
he's behaving in the most positive ways. Treat him when he's
attentive, not when he's flirting with every pretty thing within a
ten-mile radius. Indulge him when he's responsible, showing up
for engagements that he'd normally bypass if single and not
dating you. Ladies, there's a very fine line between giving him a
special new toy for the heck of it and giving him a gift when he

truly deserves it. Know the difference; otherwise, he'll trick you and expect constant special treatment without warrant. Listen, if your man thinks he can easily get what he wants all the time without making an effort, he'll take it and then leave it! Remember, most men are hunters, and they do like the chase. It's up to you to teach him that romantic candlelit nights featuring his favorite wine and dish, with you capping the evening by making a sensual move, are a treat and shouldn't be taken for granted. Let your man prove himself. Teach him to jump through a few hoops (or over several barrels) before he gets the ultimate reward . . . you! And guess what? You'll keep him running back for more and more treats if he has to work for the prize!

Housebreaking

Roll up your sleeves. You have your job cut out for you when it comes to housebreaking a man. Men and dogs both mark their territory. Dogs refer back to their wild ancestors, claiming their territory by leaving scent marks and relieving themselves at home in the yard. Modern men claim their territory by leaving worn socks, wet towels, and dirty clothes on the floor, the back of a chair, or the end of the bed. Neither men nor dogs do dishes or laundry or put the toilet seat down. Both are terrified by the sound of vacuum cleaners. Actually, what your man is doing is possessively claiming his right to be leader of the pack, king of the jungle, and head of the den, ultimately scaring away any other men who might dare to threaten his domain. First step: When he does leave his clothes and wet towels thrown around your home, tell him "No" immediately. Next: Suggest that he pick up after himself right away, leaving less of a mess for later. Don't rub his nose in it; instead, pet and praise him when he does clean up after himself without prompting. Create routines when it comes to housebreaking your main squeeze, no matter how much he barks and whines about it.

We've all heard the true saying "You can't teach an old dog new tricks." Take a deep breath and call on your strength, whether you're marrying a confirmed bachelor, living with a man whose previous girlfriend let him get away with murder, or newly cohabiting with a mama's boy. You'll have to create and enforce house rules more rigorously and consistently than you would with a puppy. Your saving grace is that men and dogs like to have a designated space they can claim as their own. Take the initiative and create a special room for him, whether it be a den, workroom, game room, or any place that he can call his own and mess up as often as he likes. Don't put him in the doghouse unless he deserves it! The irony of it all is that his special room is the one room that he'll probably keep immaculate!

The Leash

Men and dogs are similar; some are easier to train and keep on a leash, while others take a little more patience and perseverance to train. You'll determine the length of leash you need right from the beginning of your relationship. Start by

keeping your man on a tight leash, close to your side, until he learns to walk beside you, not in front of or behind you. Here's the trick for when you're not with him: Ease up on the grip and he'll find himself missing the tight hold. When you're apart, give him more rope (and hope he won't choke himself), and it will build trust between the two of you. You know the time is right to let the leash out a little when

you're on the beach and he has eyes for your legs only, while rubbing suntan lotion all over you! Ladies, remember: Men will always be dogs, so you can never take them off the leash completely!

Jealousy

The green-eyed monster strikes men and dogs alike! Men's emotions are obviously more complex than those of dogs. But jealousy emerges when both feel insecure or threatened and have to compete for more attention. The training tip here is to tame your man's aroused jealousy by reassuring him and offering him an extra expression of affection. An unexpected kiss, hug, night on the town, or tickets to his favorite sporting event will make him feel special and appreciated. If an ex shows up at a social setting and starts talking to you about the good old days, and your present steady date starts to shows signs of jealousy, don't discuss it until you get home. Don't put him on the spot, or he might feel more territorially threatened and start a dogfight! You'll have more success calming your man when the object of his competition isn't around. Jealousy can cause aggressiveness. Encourage your main squeeze to exercise daily at the gym or participate in healthy physical activity to positively channel any misplaced anger. If he's more confident, he'll conquer feelings of inadequacy, keep jealousy at bay, and hold you closer.

Touching

Petting men and dogs is equally important, because it encourages pleasurable affectionate responses from both. Touching, massaging, running your hands through your man's hair, playfully scratching his back, and nurturing in general will strengthen the bond between you and make him feel happy and secure. If the man in your life has been hurt or mistreated in a past relationship, constant reassurance and touching will mend his heartbreak and heal old wounds. Touching will promote trust within your relationship. When your man experiences trust with you, he will carry it to the outside world, thinking that it's not such a scary place out there! He'll benefit socially and professionally from having this loving, affectionate connection with you. Don't forget: If he's financially successful, that means he'll bring home a bone or two to share with you. Off you go to the hairdresser, health spa, and boutique for an overall grooming session!

Problem Barking

The two primary reasons that men and dogs bark, howl, and whine are normal insecurity and separation anxiety. Have you noticed that a man will have a bone to pick with you when you're going on a girl's night out or business trip or visiting family and friends without him? However annoying, it's his unique way of telling you he doesn't want you to leave. When he starts barking unreasonably, use the No

command. Then reassure him by touching—a hug, a kiss, or some other affectionate gesture. Make it perfectly clear that he has absolutely nothing to worry about. You will return! If your husband or boyfriend begins to whine when you ask him to participate in household chores, reassure him that the vacuum won't hurt him!

CHAPTER FOUR

Success Stories

"A dog is one of the remaining reasons why some people can be persuaded to go for a walk."

O. A. BATTISTA

What's a book about dating, romance, love, and marriage without a few happy endings? This chapter provides success stories that are doggone funny . . . and will reveal the positive effect that dogs can have on your life. I reveal how dogs have altered the fates of different people and situations, teaching us that we should never downplay the importance of the cute canines that were destined to be in our lives. The heartwarming stories will surely make you bark out loud when you read about the antics and love inspiration the dogs offered! Men planning to propose to their girlfriends are always looking for unique and clever ways to do it. I share with you some of the most doggone-friendly marriage proposals and

126

one that went awry but turned into a happy ending at the last fateful moment. Not only will these success stories entertain you, but they can also provide the man in your life with some creative new ideas on how he can include his dog when he decides to pop the question, plan a special anniversary celebration, or present you with a unique holiday gift. Curious? Read on!

Heather and Frank

Frank and his girlfriend, Heather, had dated for about five years when he finally got up the nerve to ask for her hand in marriage. They had known for years that they wanted a dog, and Frank thought that this would be the perfect opportunity to combine two fabulous life-altering choices. He discovered that miniature schnauzers tickled Heather's fancy. Schnauzers are loving, devoted, protective, enthusiastic, and patient with children. Frank set off to find a responsible breeder. He did his research and found a breeder in upstate New York. The schnauzer puppies would be ready for a new home in about a month, which gave Frank time to purchase the engagement ring and put his plan in motion.

On the sly, Frank went upstate and chose the most adorable puppy in the litter. He gave the breeder a special tag and collar to be worn by the puppy on the day he scheduled to pick up the furry bundle of joy. Frank's plan was gaining momentum!

A month later Frank and Heather drove upstate for what she thought was a casual ride in the country. Frank had purchased a beautiful engagement ring for Heather and had kept the puppy a secret surprise for her. They passed the breeder's house, which had a sign out front reading PUPPIES FOR SALE. Frank insisted that they pull over. The breeder brought the puppy out and handed it to Heather. She could hardly hide her excitement when she saw the miniature schnauzer pup. She read the tag around his neck: HEATHER, WILL YOU MARRY ME? After a moment of confusion, Frank was on one knee, Heather was crying, and the pup was licking her face. Heather later remarked, "Having Junior participate in my engagement to Frank was the most memorable moment of my life!"

Pam and Larry

Pam and Larry's success story had many twists and turns before it was a complete success. Larry wished his proposal went as smoothly as Frank's had. Larry had the original idea of using his Yorkshire terrier, Hank, to pop the question to his girlfriend, Pam. Yorkies are spunky, stubborn dogs who like to be in the center of all activities. In anticipation of her homecoming from a successful business trip, Larry tied the wedding ring with a thin white ribbon around Hank's neck. Pam called Larry to let him know that she would be a little late arriving home. When Larry turned around to take the ring from around the dog's neck, the ring and the ribbon were gone! Larry frantically searched the apartment, coming to the realization that Hank must have chewed through the ribbon and swallowed the ring. He quickly put Hank in the car, and just as he was about to pull out of the driveway, Pam returned home. When she asked Larry what had happened, he told her that Hank had swallowed some aspirin and he was taking him to have his stomach pumped. He didn't want to give away the fact that he was getting ready to propose to her and Hank had swallowed the ring!

A concerned Pam jumped into the car, and they were off to the veterinary hospital. At the hospital, Larry insisted on speaking with the veterinarian alone, claiming that Pam was too hysterical to participate. The doctor took X-rays and located the ring smack in the middle of Hank's stomach. Larry sighed with relief when the doctor assured him that the dog would be fine. A worried Pam was led into the examining room. With the X-ray lit up on the screen, Larry pointed out the ring in Hank's stomach. Larry then got down on one knee and proposed to Pam. Pam was thrilled and told Larry she was sure the ring was beautiful and couldn't wait to have it out of Hank's stomach and on her finger! Pam, Larry, and Hank lived happily ever after.

Stephanie and Glenn

Stephanie and Glenn had dated for seven years when Glenn decided the time was right to make it official. Glenn knew that he wanted their golden retriever, Caesar, to be an integral part of their engagement. Golden retrievers are smart dogs and can be trained easily. Caesar, being a creature of habit, always buried the same bone in the same spot in their backyard. This gave Glenn a brilliant idea! He searched in antique shops and flea markets for an antique wooden box until he found just the one he was looking for. Glenn engraved I LOVE YOU, SWEETHEART— WILL YOU MARRY ME? on the outside of the antique box. He quickly buried the box with the engagement ring and Caesar's favorite bone secured inside. Right on time, Caesar began to dig. Glenn anxiously called to Stephanie to come quickly, that Caesar had dug up something very interesting.

Stephanie and Glenn stood by while Caesar dug and scratched at the box. Stephanie bent down to see what it was. Glenn told her to pick it up and find out what was inside. Stephanie was mortified and said it was probably the coffin of someone's dead hamster. Glenn picked up the box, rubbed the dirt off the top, and read the engraving out loud to Stephanie. She wondered whose it was and how long it had been there. When Stephanie opened the box and saw Caesar's bone and a beautiful diamond and sapphire wedding ring, she laughed and then cried. "It was so within Glenn's character to propose engagement using Caesar in a funny and touching way," Stephanie laughed. Stephanie and Glenn saved Caesar's favorite bone for posterity. Caesar ran off with the box, and it didn't fare as well!

CHAPTER FIVE

Places to Rescue Your Perfect Dog

The following is a directory of credible and well-established animal organizations throughout the United States and Puerto Rico. The locations and contact information will aid you in your search for a new canine companion. You should have a keener sense of what dog best suits you after reading the characteristics and personalities of each breed. Whether you're looking for a playful, entertaining pup, a loyal, protective pooch, or a perfect family dog, by contacting these organizations you will be sure to find the dog of your dreams. Good luck, and have fun in your quest for that lucky dog!

United States

Save Our Strays
www.saveourstrays.com

Alabama

The Greater Birmingham Humane
Society
300 Snow Dr.
Birmingham, AL 35209
205-942-1211
www.gbhs.org

Humane Society of Etowah County
1700 Chestnut St.
Gadsden, AL 35901
256-547-4846
humanesocietyetowahcounty.org

Arizona

Arizona Humane Society
1521 W. Dobbins Rd.
Phoenix, AZ 85041
602-997-7586
www.azhumane.org

Humane Society of Southern Arizona
3540 North Kelvin Blvd.
Tucson, AZ 85716
520-327-6088
www.humane-so-arizona.org

Arkansas

Humane Society of Palaski County
14600 Colonel
Glenn Rd.
Little Rock, AR 72210
501-227-6166
www.warmhearts.org

Northeast Arkansas Humane Society
6111 East Highland Dr.
Jonesboro, AR 72401
870-932-5185
www.neahs.org

California

The Amanda Foundation
310-278-2935
www.amanda-fnd.org

Los Angeles SPCA
5026 W. Jefferson Blvd.
Los Angeles, CA 90016
323-730-5333, ext. 251
888-SPCALA1
www.spcala.org

Much Love Animal Rescue
P.O. Box 341721
Los Angeles, CA
90034-1721
310-636-9115
www.muchlove.org

San Diego Humane Society and SPCA
5500 Gaines St.
San Diego, CA 92110
619-299-7012, ext. 2249
www.sdhumane.org

Peninsula Humane Society and SPCA
12 Airport Blvd.
San Mateo, CA 94401
650-340-7022
www.peninsula
humanesociety.org/

San Francisco SPCA
2500 16th St.
San Francisco, CA 94103-4213
415-554-3000
www.sfspca.org

Sparky and the Gang
310-364-3668
sparkyandthegang@
excite.com
www.petfinder.org/shelters/CA270.html

Colorado

Denver Dumb Friends League-Humane
Society of Denver-West Shelter
2080 South Quebec St.
Denver, CO 80231
303-696-4941
303-751-5772
http://www.ddfl.org

Connecticut

Connecticut Humane Society
701 Russell Rd.
Newington, CT 06111
860-594-4500
www.cthumane.org

The Westport Shelter
455 Post Rd. East
Westport, CT
06880-4435
203-227-4137

Delaware

Delaware SPCA
Newcastle County Shelter
455 Stanton
Christiana Rd.
Newark, DE 19713
302-998-2281
www.delspca.org

Florida

Humane Society of Greater Miami
2101 N.W. 95th St.
Miami, FL 33147
305-696-0800
786-924-5220
www.humane
societymiami.org/

South Shelter
16601 SW 117th Ave.
Miami, FL 33177
305-252-3389

Jacksonville Humane Society
8464 Beach Blvd.
Jacksonville, FL 32216
904-725-8766
www.jaxhumane.org

SPCA of Central Florida
Orlando/Orange County Shelter
2727 Conroy Rd.
Orlando, FL 32839
407-351-7722
www.ohs-spca.org

Georgia

Atlanta Humane Society and SPCA
981 Howell Mill Rd. N.W.
Atlanta, GA
30318-5562
404-875-5331
www.atlhumane.org

Humane Society Chatham/Savannah
7215 Salle Mood Dr.
Savannah, GA 31406
912-354-9515
www.savannah-humane.com

Hawaii

Hawaiian Humane Society
2700 Waialae Ave.
Honolulu, HI 96826
808-946-2187
www.hawaiianhumane.org

Maui Humane Society
Mokulele Hwy.
Pu'unene, HI 96784
808-877-3680
www.mauihumane.org

Idaho

Bannock County Humane Society
P.O. Box 332
Pocatello, ID 83204
208-232-0371
www.bannockhumanesociety.org

Idaho Humane Society
4775 W. Doorman St.
Boise, ID 83705
208-342-3508, ext. 0
www.idahohumane
society.com

Illinois

The Anti-Cruelty Society
510 N. LaSalle
Chicago, IL 60610
312-644-8338
www.anticruelty.org

Chicago Humane Center-Red Door
P. O. Box 269119
Chicago, IL 60626
773-764-2242
www.reddoorshelter.org

Humane Society of Central Illinois Pet Adoption Center
3001 Gill St.
Bloomington, IL
61704-9638
309-664-7387
www.hscipets.org

Paws Chicago
3516 W. 26th Street
Chicago, IL 60623
773-521-1408
www.pawschicago.org

Indiana

Humane Society of Indianapolis
7929 North
Michigan Rd.
Indianapolis, IN 46268
317-872-5650
www.indyhumane.org

The Humane Society of Jackson County
P.O. Box 135
Seymour, IN 47274
812-522-5200
www.jchumane.org

Kansas

The Humane Society of Greater Kansas City
5445 Parallel Pkwy.
Kansas City, KS 66104
913-596-1000
www.hsgkc.org

Helping Hands Humane Society, Inc.
2625 N.W. Rochester Rd.
Topeka, KS
66617-1201
785-233-7325
www.topekahumaneshelter.org

Kentucky

Kentucky Humane Society "Lifelong Friends"
241 Steedly Dr.
Louisville, KY 40214
502-366-3355
www.kyhumane.org

Woodford Humane Society
P.O. Box 44
Versailles, KY 40383
859-873-5491
www.woodford
humanesociety.org

Louisiana

Iberia Humane Society "Have a Heart"
P.O. Box 11422
New Iberia, LA
70562-1422
318-365-1923
www.iberiahumane.com

St. Tammany Humane Society
20384 Harrison Ave.
Covington, LA 70433
985-893-9474, ext. 6

New Orleans SPCA
1319 Japonica St.
New Orleans, LA 70117
504-944-7445
www.la-spca.org

Maine

Greater Androscoggin Humane Society
3312 Hotel Rd.
Auburn, ME 04210
207-783-2311
www.gahumane.org

Humane Society of Knox County
P.O. Box 1294
Rockland, ME 04841
207-594-2200
www.humanesocietyofknoxcounty.org

Maryland

Fredrick County Humane Society
5712 D Industry Ln.
Frederick, MD 21704
301-694-8300
www.fchs.org

Maryland SPCA
3300 Falls Rd.
Baltimore, MD 21211
410-235-8826
www.mdspca.org

Massachusetts

Animal Rescue League of Boston
10 Chandler St.
Boston, MA 02116
617-426-9170, ext. 110, ext. 169
www.arlboston.org

Massachusetts SPCA
350 South Huntington Ave.
Boston, MA 02130
617-522-7400
www.mspca.org

Northeast Animal Shelter
204 Highland Ave.
P.O. Box 4506
Salem, MA
01970-0901
978-745-9888
www.northeastanimalshelter.org

Michigan

Michigan Humane Society
www.michiganhumane.org

Detroit Shelter
7401 Chrysler Dr.
Detroit, MI 48211
313-872-3400

Rochester Hills Shelter
3600 W. Auburn Rd.
Rochester Hills, MI 48309
248-852-7420

Westland Shelter
37255 Marquette
Westland, MI 48185
734-721-7300

Minnesota

Humane Society for Companion
Animals
1115 Beulah Ln.
St. Paul, MN 55108
651-645-7387
http://www.hsca.net/

Northwoods Humane Society
9785 Hudson Rd.
Woodbury, MN 55125
651-730-6008
www.northwoodshs.org

Mississippi

Humane Society of South Mississippi
13756 Washington Ave.
Gulfport, MS 39503
228-863-4394
www.hssm.org

Pearl River County SPCA
P.O. Box 191
Picayune, MS 39466
601-798-8000
www.prcspca.org

Missouri

Animal Protection Agency
1705 S. Hanley Rd.
Brentwood, MO 63144-2909
314-645-4610, ext. 21

Humane Society of Missouri
St. Louis Adoption Center
1201 Macklind Ave.
St. Louis, MO 63110
314-951-1562
www.hsmo.org

Westport Area Branch Adoption Center
2400 Drilling Service Rd.
Maryland Heights, MO 63043
314-951-1588

Montana

Humane Society of Gallatin Valley
P.O. Box 11390
Bozeman, MT 59719
hsofgv@imt.net

Montana Pets on the Net
Rimrock Humane Society
P.O. Box 834
Roundup, MT 59072
406-323-3687
www.montanapets.org

Nebraska

Central Nebraska Humane Society
1312 Sky Park Rd.
Grand Island, NE 68801
308-385-5305
members.petfinder.org/~NE13/

Nebraska Humane Society
8929 Fort St.
Omaha, NE
68134-2899
402-444-7800
www.nehumanesociety.org

Nevada

Nevada Humane Society
200 Kresge Ln.
Sparks, NV 89431
775-331-5770
www.nevadahumanesociety.org/

New Hampshire

New Hampshire Humane Society
1305 Meredith Center Rd.
Laconia, NH 03246
603-524-3252
www.nhhumane.org/

New Jersey

Mt. Pleasant Animal Shelter
194 Route 10 West
East Hanover, NJ 07936
973-386-0590
www.njshelter.org

New Mexico

Heart and Soul Animal Sanctuary
369 Montezuma Ave., #130
Santa Fe, NM 87501
505-757-6817
www.animal-sanctuary.org

Humane Society of
Taos, Inc.
P.O. Box 622
Taos, NM 87571
505-758-9708
www.joycefay.com/taos/index.shtml

New York

Animal Rescue Fund of the Hamptons
P.O. Box 901
Wainscott, NY 11975
631-537-0400
www.arfhamptons.org

ASCPA
424 East 92nd St.
New York, NY 10128
212-876-7700
www.aspca.org

Central Park SPCA
5878 East Molloy Rd.
Syracuse, NY 1321
315-454-4479
www.communitysite.com/SPCA

SPCA of Westchester
590 North State Rd.
Briarcliff Manor, NY 10510
914-941-2894
www.spca914.com

Suffolk County SPCA
363 Route 11
Smithtown, NY 11787
631-382-SPCA
www.suffolkspca.org

Green Chimneys Children's Services
and Green Chimneys School
(featuring human-animal interactions)
400 Doansburg Rd., Box 719
Brewster, NY 10509
845-279-2995
www.greenchimneys.org

Humane Society for Greater Nashua
24 Ferry Rd.
Nashua, NY
03064-8109
603-889-BARK (2275)
www.hsfn.org

Humane Society of
New York
306 East 59th St.
New York, NY 10022
212-752-4842
www.humanesocietyny.org

Paul Sorvino's DogFellas
212-369-2942
www.dogfellas.net

Stray from the Heart
P.O. Box 11
New York, NY
10024-0011
212-726-DOGS
www.strayfromtheheart.org

North Carolina

Humane Society of Charlotte
2700 Toomey Ave.
Charlotte, NC 28203
704-377-0534
www.clthumane.org

SPCA of Cumberland County
3232 Bragg Blvd.
Fayetteville, NC 28303
910-860-1177
www.spcaofcumberlandco.bizland.com

North Dakota

The Natural Pet Center
1307 14th Ave. South
Fargo, ND 58503
701-239-0110

Pet Connection Humane Society
730 Highway 1804 .N.E
Bismarck, ND 58503
701-222-2719
www.petcon.org

Ohio

Geauga Humane Society Cleveland
Capital Area Humane Society
(Central Ohio)
3015 Scioto-Darby Executive Ct.
Hillard, OH 43026
614-777-PETS
www.cahs-pets.org

Humane Society of Allen County
3606 Elida Rd.
Lima, OH 45807
419-991-1775
www.hsoac.org

Oklahoma

Humane Society of Stillwater
1710 South Main St.
Stillwater, OK 74074
405-377-1701
www.hspets.org

Pets and People Humane Society
701 Inla Ave.
Yukon, OK 73085
405-350-PETS
www.petsandpeople.com

Oregon

Humane Society of Central Oregon
61170 S.E. 27th St.
Bend, OR 97702
541-382-3537
www.hsco.org

Oregon Humane Society
1067 N.E. Columbia Blvd.
Portland, OR 97211
503-282-7722
www.oregonhumane.org

Pennsylvania

Pennsylvania SPCA
350 E. Erie Ave.
Philadelphia, PA 19134
www.pspca.org

Animal Friends
2643 Penn Ave.
Pittsburgh, PA 15222
412-566-2100
www.animal-friends.org

Morris Animal Refuge
1242 Lombard St.
Philadelphia, PA 19147
215-735-3256
215-735-9570
www.morrisanimalrefuge.org

Puerto Rico

Fundación Save a Sato
Villas de Cappara, D-2 Calle C
Guaynabo, Puerto Rico 00966
www.saveasato.org

Rhode Island

Providence Animal Rescue League
34 Elbow St.
Providence, RI 02903
401-421-1399
www.parl.org

Animal Rescue League of Southern
Rhode Island
P.O. Box 458
Wakefield, RI
02880-0458
www.southkingstown.com/arl/

South Carolina

John Ancrum SPCA
3861 Leeds Ave.
Charleston, SC 29405
843-747-4849
www.jaspca.com

Oconee County Humane Society
321 Camp Rd.
Walhalla, SC
29691-4811
864-638-8798
www.oconeehumane.org

South Dakota

Aberdeen Area Humane Society
P.O. Box 1013
Aberdeen, SD
57402-1013
605-266-1200
www.anewleashonlife.net

Sioux Falls Area Humane Society
3720 East Benson Rd.
Sioux Falls, SD 57104
605-338-4441
www.sfhumanesociety.com

Tennessee

The Humane Society of the
Tennessee Valley, South Knoxville
Adoption Center
P.O. Box 9479
Knoxville, TN 37940
865-573-9675
www.humanesocietytennessee.com

Texas

SPCA of Texas
362 S. Industrial Blvd.
Dallas, TX 75207
214-651-9611
1-888-ANIMALS
www.spca.org

Dog and Kitty City/Humane
Society of Dallas
2719 Manor Way
Dallas, TX 75235
214-350-7387
www.dognkittycity.com

Austin Humane Society
124 W. Anderson Ln.
Austin, TX 78752
512-837-7985
www.austinspca.com

Houston SPCA
900 Portway Dr.
Houston, TX 77024
713-869-SPCA (7722)
www.spcahouston.org

Martin Spay/Neuter Clinic
362 S. Industrial Blvd.
Dallas, TX 75207

Utah

Best Friends Animal Society
5001 Angel Canyon Rd.
Kanab, UT
84741-5000
435-644-2001
www.bestfriends.org

Community Animal Welfare Society
(CAWS)
P.O. Box 17825
Salt Lake City, UT 84117
801-328-4731
www.caws.org

Humane Society of Utah
P.O. Box 573659
Murray, UT
84157-3659
801-261-2919
www.utahhumane.org

Vermont

Addison County Humane Society
236 Boardman St.
Middlebury, VT 05753
802-388-1100
www.addisonhumane.org

Frontier Animal Society of Vermont
4473 Barton
Orleans Rd.
Orleans, VT 05860
802-754-2228
www.frontieranimalsociety.com

Virginia

Richmond SPCA
2519 Hermitage Rd.
Richmond, VA 23220
804-643-6785
www.richmondspca.org

Virginia Beach SPCA
3040 Holland Rd.
Virginia Beach, VA 23453
757-427-0070
www.vbspca.com

Washington

The Humane Society for Seattle/King
County
13212 S.E. Eastgate Way
Bellevue, WA 98005
425-641-0800
www.seattlehumane.org

Seattle Animal Shelter
2061 15th Ave. West
Seattle, WA 98119
206-386-PETS
www.ci.seattle.wa.us/animalshelter/

Humane Society for Southwest
Washington
2121 St. Francis Lane
Vancouver, WA 98660
360-693-4746
www.southwesthumane.org

Washington, D.C.

Washington Animal Rescue League
71 Oglethorpe St., N.W.
Washington, D.C. 20011
202-726-2556
www.warl.org

Washington Humane Society
1201 New York Ave., N.E.
Washington, DC 20002
202-576-6664
or
7319 Georgia Ave., N.W.
Washington, DC 20012
202-BE-HUMANE
www.washhumane.org

West Virginia

Berkeley County Humane Society
554 Charles Town Rd.
Martinsburg, WV 25401
304-267-8389
berkeley.wvhumane.com

Kanawha/Charleston Humane
Association
1248 Greenbrier St.
Charleston, WV 25311
304-342-1576
www.wvanimalshelter.com

Wisconsin

Chippewa County Humane Association
10503 CTH S South
Chippewa Falls, WI 54729
715-382-4832
www.chippewahumane.com

Forest County Humane Society
701 Industrial Pky.
Crandon, WI 54520
715-478-2098
www.petfinder.org/shelters/WI62.html

Wyoming

Lander Pet
Connections, Inc.
385 Del St.
Lander, WY 82520
www.webpan.com/petconnection

Wendy Diamond is the founder and the editorial director of *Animal Fair* (fairness to animals), a lifestyle magazine for pet owners. Her other accomplishments include two best-selling cookbooks, *A Musical Feast* and *An All-Star Feast*, featuring recipes donated by celebrities and athletes, which benefited charities. She is a leading authority on animal lifestyles, and in 2002, she starred in the critically acclaimed TV show *Single in the City*, where she and Lucky went off in search of Mr. Right Breed.

Wendy was born in Chagrin Falls, Ohio, and currently lives in New York with Pasha, her Russian blue rescued cat, and Lucky, her six-pound Maltese. And she's still searching for that lucky Mr. Right. For more information, please visit www.animalfair.com.